LEISURE ARTS

Vice President and Editor-in-Chief:
  Sandra Graham Case
Executive Publications Director:
  Cheryl Nodine Gunnells
Senior Publications Director: Susan White Sullivan
Designer Relations Director: Debra Nettles
Craft Publications Director: Deb Moore
Senior Design Director: Cyndi Hansen
Special Projects Director: Susan Frantz Wiles
Senior Prepress Director: Mark Hawkins

EDITORIAL STAFF
TECHNICAL
Project Writer: Laura Siar Holyfield
Project Writing Associate: Christina Kirkendoll

EDITORIAL
Writers: Deb Moore and Susan McManus Johnson

DESIGN
Designers: Kim Kern, Kelly Reider, Anne Pulliam Stocks,
  Lori Wenger, and Becky Werle
Contributing Designer: Tonya Bradford Bates

ART
Art Publications Director: Rhonda Shelby
Art Category Manager: Lora Puls
Lead Graphic Artist: Dayle Carozza
Graphic Artists: Amy Gerke, Dana Vaughn,
  Janie Wright, and Jeanne Zaffarano
Imaging Technicians: Brian Hall, Stephanie Johnson,
  and Mark R. Potter
Photography Manager: Katherine Atchison
Photo Stylists: Cyndi Hansen and Kim Kern
Publishing Systems Administrator: Becky Riddle
Publishing Systems Assistants: Clint Hanson and
  John Rose

BUSINESS STAFF
Vice President and Chief Operations Officer:
  Tom Siebenmorgen
Corporate Planning and Development Director:
  Laticia Mull Dittrich
Vice President, Sales and Marketing: Pam Stebbins
National Accounts Director: Martha Adams
Sales and Services Director: Margaret Reinold
Vice President, Operations: Jim Dittrich
Comptroller, Operations: Rob Thieme
Retail Customer Service Manager: Stan Raynor
Print Production Manager: Fred F. Pruss

A special thanks to Ken West Photography of Little
  Rock, Arkansas.

Library of Congress Catalog Number 20-07923925
Hardcover ISBN-10: 1-60140-589-8

10 9 8 7 6 5 4 3 2 1

table of contents

Welcome to *trimmings: the art of holiday living*.

It's a special kind of book, and not like any you've seen from us before. When our Editor-in-Chief, Sandra, asked if the Design Team would be interested in developing a different kind of Christmas book, I knew the answer right away. The team had been searching for a project specifically aimed at today's crafter—that intrepid soul who doesn't always care if instructions are followed to the letter. We've known for some time now that crafters today are more about putting their own spin on a project and making it their own.

And Leisure Arts' designers are all about a challenge. So when we told them that they could use any material or technique in any way they wanted, they broke the sound barrier coming up with new ideas. But don't worry. If you aren't ready to strike out on your own, we've included patterns and specific instructions for you to recreate the projects you'll find here. We just want you to make something.

It's up to you to make it yours.

Cyndi

A quick thank-you to Tonya Bates, a valued designer who transferred with her husband to another city after the book was begun. Tonya was instrumental in concepting the book, and her elf design can be seen on page 12.

cyndi Leisure Arts' Senior Director of Design has been making her living in the craft field for over twenty years. She's passionate about the work, but cares even more deeply about perpetuating the love of crafting in others—especially when it comes to encouraging them to try something new.

"Everyone has an inner artist. My favorite part of the job is helping the reader embrace her creativity and let that artist out."

Cyndi's background includes stints in ceramics, floral design, and home décor. Along the way, she published a children's party guide, made a few television appearances, and for the past ten years, has been instrumental in many, many craft publications.

"I'm a big believer in putting your stamp on the things that fill your world. It's very rewarding, even if the things you make aren't picture-perfect. They're yours—what could be more perfect than that?"

Dedicated to the artist in each of us.

anne was inspired and encouraged by family members and their craft. Her great-grandmother was a serious quilter, her grandmother an embroidery expert, her mother a seamstress and needlepoint teacher, and her father a woodworker and furniture maker.

Although Anne studied elementary education, her job choices reflect her love of fiber, texture and color. Her work at a designer fabric shop led to an interest in working with beautiful fabrics to create unique and inspired living spaces. When the opportunity came to join the team at Leisure Arts and "work with people who share my passion for a piece of fabric or wonderful yarn," she jumped at it.

becky has always felt the urge to create and considers it her dominant trait. Eager for the weekly art class in elementary school, she continued to pursue the thrill in later years, garnering a degree in art education. After teaching art for 6 years (including an enriching stint in the Peace Corps), she realized that she was happiest when pursuing her own creations.

Inspiration comes in the form of other artists' work, their studio spaces, or seeing an amazing piece in a book or magazine article. "I start thinking about the ways I would make something like that. What follows next is challenging myself to change it enough to make it my own, letting the inspiration take me to another dimension." While Becky enjoys virtually all forms of crafts, she gets the biggest rush when trying new things.

kelly credits her mother with starting her on her current path. "Mom was always trying something new, and she taught me to sew when I was very small." Since then, Kelly has used just about every craft/art medium that exists—and loves it all—but her favorite continues to be cloth, which she sews and manipulates into art dolls and figures.

Kelly is inspired by a love of color and movement, so it's no surprise that she's thrilled when the end result of a project is different than anticipated. "The unexpected is my favorite aspect of any project, whether it's my own—or someone else's. For me, there's great emotion and satisfaction in making things—in seeing what is there and making it mine."

kim

has a BA in Studio Art from Ouachita Baptist University, but credits her family with encouraging her to pursue her life-long dream of becoming a working artist.

Like most creative types, Kim is happiest when creating, but she doesn't sit and wait for inspiration to strike. "If I don't have a project going, I swim through magazines until something jumps out at me. I think, 'Hey! I can make something like that!' Then my brain is working!"

Kim is inspired by vivid, "feel-good" colors, reflected in her magpie-bright and cheery designs.

lori

has a BA in Studio Art and a background in magazine illustration, and even does some photo styling for Leisure Arts' publications. This latter experience enables her to really get outside her projects and see them the way others will. Perhaps because of this, she loves introducing the unexpected into her designs. "I look for ways to add a surprise element, because I love that 'Oh!' response."

Lori is as comfortable in front of the camera as behind the scenes, and co-hosts Leisure Arts' new DVD, *Style Remix.*

adorn

Dressing the house for the holidays is the official launch of the season. And even though you may perform the same tasks every year—bringing the decorations down from the attic, unpacking the ornaments, detangling the lights, shifting the furniture to make room for the tree—the transformation is always wondrous, always surprising.

Because you always introduce something new.

Here are some new takes on the old holiday traditions: Three non-standard stockings for gifts of good cheer. *Objets d'art* and ornaments fashioned from surprisingly common elements. A tree skirt trimmed in purple ribbons to greet a blissful New Year. And a quintuplet of paper clay characters to shape as you please—as many as you want.

santa and company

In each chapter of *trimmings*, we issued a challenge to our designers: Thrill us with your individual take on the very same project. And thrill us they did.

Each designer challenge serves two purposes—to illustrate how many different ways there are to tackle one design, and to encourage you to let your personality shine through as you approach the projects in this book.

You definitely need to try this project—then you may need professional help to quit. After our designers came up with the members of this little troupe, they were hooked—and one headed home to make some more. Her neighbors and their children wandered by and everyone got in on the act. You'll find that your characters will develop distinctive personalities, each one a star among stars. Turn the page for more about our designers' unique cast of characters (and to think they each began with the same foam shapes and dowel rods). For the basic supplies and how to assemble the figures, see *About Santa and Company* on page 110. Take it from there and discover who steps out of your imagination.

suspendered animation

A natural at set construction, Tonya's elf is making a guest appearance from the North Pole (or thereabouts).

After painting the clay elf, apply Snow-Tex to the base. Glue rattail suspenders and buttons to the elf. Glue tufts of floss to his head (Tonya chose carrot orange hair for her elf). Paint the boxes or cover them with scrapbook paper and tie them up with cord.

✳ Snow-Tex™ textural medium
✳ Rattail ✳ Four ¼" dia. buttons
✳ Embroidery floss ✳ 2⅜" dia. and 2½" square papier-mâché boxes
✳ Scrapbook paper (optional)
✳ Metallic wired cord

paisley santa

Only the star of the show could get away with an outfit like this. Lori saw the pattern on scrapbook paper and liked the silly image of Santa wearing pink paisley.

Add a cone-shaped hat to your Santa as you cover the framework with clay (Lori cut hers from scrapbook paper). After painting, glue pom-poms around the base of the hat and on the boots. Glue the ribbon around Santa's middle and add a glittered star.

✳ Scrapbook paper ✳ Green metallic pom-poms ✳ ⅜" wide black velvet ribbon ✳ Star cut from Creative Paperclay®, painted and glittered

santa wanna-be

The bewhiskered snowman is an eager understudy and hopes to play the part of Santa someday. The idea of Santa's beard on a snowman cracked Kelly up and she had to try it out.

Apply Snow-Tex to the base of the painted snowman. Tie a flannel scarf around his neck (Kelly glued fringed felt to the bottom edges of her scarf). Cut a beard from faux fur. Thread pieces of string through the top corners of the beard; glue the string to the back of the head. Fashion a Santa hat from felt and a pom-pom and spot glue it in place.

✳ Snow-Tex™ textural medium ✳ Blue printed flannel ✳ Blue, red, and white felt scraps ✳ White faux fur scrap ✳ Sharp needle ✳ White string ✳ White pom-pom

crafty santa

Taking his cue from a papier-mâché Halloween figure, Becky's Santa shows versatility by drawing from other holidays for Christmas inspiration.

Drill a hole through both ends of the dowel arms. Prepare Santa's framework (Becky cut her hat and boots from a foam ball and covered them with clay). After painting, glue on a yarn beard and cuffs. Add felt buttons with white thread knots for the holes. Glue on a buckle cut from tooling foil. Wire a star and wreath to Santa's hands. Glue the pom-pom to the hat and a scalloped felt strip around the base.

✳ Craft knife and cutting mat ✳ Additional foam ball ✳ White novelty yarn ✳ Black felt scrap ✳ White thread ✳ Aluminum tooling foil ✳ Medium-gauge wire ✳ Star and wreath (Becky cut hers from Creative Paperclay®; then, added glitter to the star and beads to the wreath) ✳ White pom-pom ✳ Scallop-edged scissors ✳ Red felt

glitzen

Nothing holds the show together like glitter and Glitzen. There's a saying among the designers that if you don't keep moving, Kim will glitter you. She agrees, "Glitter is my inspiration!"

Drill a hole through both ends of the dowel arms and prepare the reindeer's framework. Shape antlers from armature wire wrapped with floral tape and insert them into the head. Paint the figure. (Kim made a vest from felt and wrapped it around the reindeer. Then she attached the arms, poking the wire through the vest into the body.) Brush glue wherever you want the glitter to land and sprinkle with glitter (Kim added it to the antlers, nose, hooves, letters, and base). Poke a hole through the top of each letter and attach a jump ring. Thread the rings onto an 8" wire length, adding bells between letters. Tie short pieces of ribbon here and there along the wire. Thread the wire ends through the hoof holes and secure. Fashion a bridle and reins from metallic cord and brads, gluing the cord ends behind the brads. Add a message to the base.

✳ 1/8" dia. armature wire ✳ Floral tape ✳ Printed felt ✳ Old paintbrush ✳ Assorted colors of glitter ✳ Cardboard letter cutouts (ours spell "Jingle") ✳ Sharp needle ✳ Jump rings ✳ Medium-gauge wire ✳ Jingle bells ✳ ¼" wide sheer ribbon ✳ Metallic cord ✳ Brads ✳ Black permanent marker

ornament
update

Gather a few crafting standbys—beads, floss, felt, sequins—and fashion original treasures that are destined to dangle. Here are a few we came up with. We think they'll spark some ideas of your own.

not your typical partridge

Fill your pear (or pine) tree with fanciful songbirds this holiday. Freehand your designs or enlarge our patterns (page 111) to capture the chi of birds. For 7"-long birds, enlarge the bluebird to 208% and the orange bird to 108%. Cut two of each bird from felt. (We fused or stitched a fabric wing over each felt wing.) Sew on a bead or sequin eye and any motifs to the front of the bird (we zigzagged a fabric heart on the orange bird). Sew the pieces together, leaving a 1" opening (we sandwiched a pearl cotton hanging loop and the orange bird's crest between the pieces). Stuff the bird with fiberfill and sew across the opening. Glue on a beak and a wing or two, and add more beads or sequins. To give your bird a turkey loop crest (like our bluebird) see *Stitches* on page 108.

✳ Felt in assorted colors ✳ Paper-backed fusible web (optional) ✳ Patterned fabric scraps ✳ Assorted beads ✳ Sequins ✳ Pearl cotton ✳ Polyester fiberfill ✳ Fabric glue

funky felt ornament

For starters, cut different-size circles from felt; then, add beads and floss to a few of the circles. (We stacked ours in four groups.) Thread a bell and a bead on one end of a 15" wire length and twist the end to secure. String on a bead and poke the wire through one stack of circles. Sandwich the wire in the middle of the next stack and glue the circles together. Add the other circle stacks and thread a bead on the wire. Loop the wire into a hanger and twist the end near the top bead.

* Assorted colors of hand-dyed felt
* Sharp needle * Assorted beads
* Embroidery floss * Jingle bell
* Medium-gauge copper wire
* Wire cutters * Pliers * Fabric glue

dangling modifier

Drill holes through opposite sides of the napkin ring. Wrap the napkin ring and two large beads with floss; knot and tuck the ends. Leaving a 4" tail, look at the photo to thread a long piece of floss (ours is 20") through the top beads, the wrapped ring, and the center beads. Thread on beads for the dangle, wrap the tail around the end bead, and thread the tail back through all the beads and the ring. Knot the threads together for the hanger.

* Drill and bit * 2½" dia. wooden napkin ring * Assorted painted wooden beads * Two colors of variegated embroidery floss * Tapestry needle

snowbound
chalet

An avant-garde gingerbread house makes a great group project. Build it however you wish—here's how to make one like ours. Glue the tissue box to the center of the foam base. Using the pattern (page 111), cut two pieces from cardboard for the house front and back. Cutting along the dotted line, cut two cardboard rectangles for the sides. Glue the front, back, and sides to the tissue box.

Make cardboard patterns for a quirky-shaped door and three windows; cut them out, and cut each again from scrapbook paper and an additional door from craft foam. Glue the cardboard shapes to the house as a base for the door and windows. Cover the outside of the house with a thin layer of Paperclay and allow it to dry. Brush the outside (except for the windows and door) with thinned glue and sprinkle with mica glitter. Coat the foam base with Snow-Tex. Fold and paint a 6" x 9" cardboard roof and glue it to the house.

Glue the paper windows to the house and add craft foam shutters and window frames. Layer and glue the foam and paper doors to the house, and add a foam window. Glue punched paper circles to painted discs and glue these stepping stones to the base.

For the lollipops, paint the round turnings and glue them to the $1/8$" dowels. To make the two smaller trees, cut one of the cones in two and round off the edges with sandpaper. Poke and glue $3/8$" dowels into the bottom of all three trees. Cover the trees with Paperclay, adding the curls on top; let these dry. Brush the trees with thinned glue and sprinkle with colored glitter. Insert the trees and lollipops in the base (we cut small X's in the base with the craft knife). Glue pom-poms and punched cardstock snowflakes to the roof (we glued pairs of snowflakes together to make them three-dimensional) and add a pom-pom doorknob. Glue the foam plate to the bottom of the base for that cake stand look.

✳ Craft glue ✳ Square tissue box ✳ 12" dia. foam base ✳ Tracing paper ✳ Cardboard ✳ Scrapbook papers ✳ Craft foam ✳ Creative Paperclay® ✳ Foam brush ✳ Mica glitter ✳ Snow-Tex™ textural medium ✳ Acrylic paint and paintbrushes ✳ Circle and snowflake punches ✳ 1$1/4$" wood discs ✳ Two 2$1/4$" round wood turnings ✳ $1/8$" and $3/8$" dia. dowel rods, cut into 4" lengths and painted ✳ Craft knife and cutting mat ✳ Two 6"-tall foam cones ✳ Sandpaper ✳ Colored glitter ✳ Tinsel pom-poms ✳ White cardstock ✳ Round foam dinner plate

all wired
up

It's a paradox—the more wire you wrap around this little tree, the more you'll feel yourself unwind. Drill a hole through the center of the block. Paint the block and dowel and sand the block edges. Dab glue on one end of the dowel and insert it in the block. Cut an 8"-tall tree shape from cardboard. Leaving a 3" wire tail at the bottom of the tree, wrap armature wire randomly around the tree, wrapping loosely to allow the wire tree to fill out. Cut away the cardboard. Center the wire tree on the dowel and wrap the wire tail tightly around the dowel.

Wrap the tree with the gold, green, and seed bead wires, and beaded trim. Cut a 20" length of rust wire and curl one end. Thread beads on the wire, using the pliers to coil the wire every so often. Curl the other end and wrap the strand around the tree. Repeat to add several beaded rust wire strands to the tree, using different bead combinations. Wrap the star with gold wire and wire it to the tree. For ornament hangers, cut a bunch of 3" gold wire lengths. Curl one end of each, add a large bead, and hook the other end to the tree.

* Drill and ³/₈" bit * 2" square wooden block * Acrylic paint and paintbrushes * ³/₈" dia. dowel rod, cut to 11¹/₂"
* Sandpaper * Wood glue * Cardboard * 8-ft. length of ¹/₁₆" dia. armature wire * Wire cutters * Assorted colors and thicknesses of wire and beaded trim from your stash (we used 20-gauge gold wire, green coated wire, purple and gold seed bead wires, #22 rust wire, and green beaded trim) * Assorted beads (use beads from cast-off or flea market jewelry) * Needle-nose pliers * 2" wide rusty tin star

santa's
chair

Make this miniature chair from odds and ends (when Santa shows up, it magically becomes big enough for him to sit on). Begin by drilling holes near the back of the seat for the foot-long brushes to rest in. Drill two holes partway through the bottom of the seat front for the pencil "legs." (We drilled these at an angle so the pencils would flare out a bit.) Next, coat the seat with orange and red, or pick your own paints. When the seat dries, sand it here and there. Hot glue the brushes and pencils in place. Touch up the back legs with painted stripes, spots, and splashes.

Cut three slats from the yardstick for the chair back. Add rub-on sayings to the slats and the seat; then, hot glue the slats to the brushes. Tie jute around one of the brushes and glue on Santa's initials so he'll know it's just for him.

* Drill and bits * Wood scrap for seat (ours is a 4$^1/_2$" square) * Two 12"-long artist's paintbrushes * Two pencils * Acrylic paints and brushes * Sandpaper * Hot glue gun * Handsaw * Yardstick * Rub-on Christmas sayings * Black jute * Chipboard glitter letters "S" and "C"

intriguing
tree skirt

You'll smile each time you look at this tree skirt made in colors you love. Cut a fabric square or circle a little larger than your tree stand (see *Cutting a Fabric Circle* on page 110 for pointers). Cut a small hole in the center for the trunk, and cut a straight line from the center hole to the edge of the skirt for the opening. Follow the felting needle package instructions and the photos to add yarn loop fringe to the outer edge with the felting needle tool. Then layer strips of ribbon with small yarn loops on top. Use the tool to attach the yarn and ribbon to the skirt at the same time. Finish the skirt by adding a length of yarn along the center circle and opening edges.

stockings
three

Newsprint, variegated yarn, a second-hand sweater? These are just a few of the unusual materials you can use to make a kicked-up version of an old tradition.

newsprint stocking

Tear different-sized rectangles from newspaper, overlap and lightly glue them together with the glue stick to make a 13" x 22" rectangle. Zigzag stitch all over the papers in different directions. Enlarge the black stocking pattern (page 112) to 216% and use pinking shears to cut one stocking from the stitched newspaper and one in reverse from the backing fabric. Fold the cuff on the fabric piece to the wrong side and sew along the fold with a straight stitch. Trim the extra cuff fabric. Fold the newspaper cuff to the front and straight stitch along the fold; turn the cuff up. Matching wrong sides, zigzag the stocking pieces together along the sides and bottom.

For each flower, layer and accordion-fold eight 10" x 12" pieces of tissue paper into a $\frac{1}{2}$" x 12" strip. Tie a piece of wire tightly around the middle. Trim the tissue ends to a point and carefully pull the tissue toward the center, two layers at a time to make a flower. Roll a piece of tinsel into a ball and glue it to the center of the flower. Push the wire ends through the stocking and thread them through a button; then, tie off and trim the ends. Sew tissue that was trimmed from a flower under the edges of the cuff. For the hanger, sew a layered ribbon loop to the inside and back of the stocking.

✳ Newspaper ✳ Glue stick ✳ Sewing thread in bright colors ✳ Pinking shears ✳ 13" x 22" piece of backing fabric ✳ Tissue paper in assorted colors ✳ Fine-gauge wire ✳ Wire cutters ✳ Tinsel ✳ Craft glue ✳ Buttons ✳ Ribbons

just add yarn stocking

Omitting the flap, enlarge the black stocking pattern (page 112) to 216%. Use pinking shears to cut the stocking back from felt, just outside the pattern line and to cut the stocking front slightly smaller than the pattern line. Unwind the yarn randomly on the stocking front. Follow the felting needle package instructions to attach the yarn to the felt with the felting needle tool. Sew all over the stocking front. Center and sew the front to the stocking back along the sides and bottom. Attach a yarn hanger. Follow *Pom-poms* (page 109) to make 2¹/₂" dia. pom-poms to match the stocking back and attach them near the hanger.

※ Pinking shears ※ Two 13" x 18" felt pieces (ours are watermelon and cranberry colored) ※ Variegated yarn ※ Felting needle tool and mat ※ 2" cardboard square ※ Yarn to match the stocking back

sweater stocking

Turn the sweater wrong side out. Enlarge the red stocking pattern (page 112) to 210%. Cut out the stocking and pin it to the front of the sweater (the collar may extend above the pattern). Machine zigzag beside the side and bottom edges of the pattern. Cut ¹/₄" outside the stitching and turn the stocking right side out. Cut the tag from the sweater. Fuse appliqués and sew sequins to the collar.

For the hanger, fold a 3" x 12" sweater strip in half, matching the right sides and long edges. Sew the long edges and one end together, and turn right side out. Tuck the end ¹/₂" to the wrong side and sew it closed. Sew one end of the hanger to the back of the stocking and sew a hook and loop fastener to the hanger for a closure.

※ Old sweater (ours has a shawl collar) ※ Fusible sequin appliqués ※ Assorted sequins ※ Hook and loop fastener

gather

Everyone is flitting here and there at this time of year. Getting family and friends to land at your place and settle in for a real visit can be a matter of creating the right atmosphere. That's where your Christmas spirit meets your glue gun. Or your paint brush. Or scissors.

You get the idea.

And we have ideas to get you started. Check out these platters, place settings, and playful candles. Your crowd won't see these holiday artworks anywhere else. And savvy guests will know right away that you've pulled out the stops for their benefit. Only you will understand that these expressions of your talent were so much fun to make, it was no trouble at all.

Just be sure the hall tree is sturdy enough to hold lots of coats and hats for hours on end. And keep the eggnog coming.

significant platters

Each of our designers sketched an idea for a 12" holiday platter and then took off to a do-it-yourself pottery studio. They had such a great time sharing their creativity—you've just got to gather your friends and go! After the pieces are ready (usually within a week), invite your cohorts home for a platter potluck.

To get started, draw your own design, or choose from our patterns, beginning on page 113. Then grab your jacket and take along a piece of graphite paper to transfer the artwork. The shop will supply everything you need to create unique ceramic pieces. Find a nearby store in the phone book or online. Turn the page for tips from our designers, as well as an up close and personal look at each platter.

✳ Your own drawn design or a pattern enlarged to 157%
✳ Graphite transfer paper ✳ Ballpoint pen ✳ The pottery studio will supply the 12" square platter, paints, paintbrushes, and any other supplies you may need.

At the studio, choose your platter; then, wipe it with a damp sponge to remove any dust. Basecoat the platter and give it a few extra coats to intensify the color; then, let it dry. Transfer your design with a ballpoint pen and graphite paper (the lines will disappear when it's fired, even if the graphite mixes into your paint colors). Paint the design, removing any unwanted spots of color with a toothpick, and follow up with additional coats. (Use a different number of coats for varied shades of the same color.) If you like, leave white areas unpainted—like our snowman and blanket of snow.

No local studios? Just tape the pattern to the back of a clear glass plate, paint the front with glass paints, and apply a sealer. Place another clear glass plate on top to serve food.

stress-free snowman

Kelly didn't worry about drawing perfect circles to make her snowman—much of his charm is in the hand-drawn look. The scarf evolved from one hanging on the back of a nearby chair.

wintry woods

A shakeable snow globe from Kim's childhood inspired the trees and snowy hills. "Can't you just see the snow swirling around?"

holly splash

Lori created a graphic motif from the traditional holly shape. The final colors after firing came as a surprise—a part of ceramic artistry that guarantees originality.

strictly ornamental

Anne began with an appealing ornament shape, and to stretch her creative spirit, chose soft pastel colors from a fashion magazine. She painted sparkles and dots with a fine-tip squeeze bottle.

by the chimney

Becky chose her theme from the classic Christmas poem and found her colors in holiday displays at a favorite store.

swag
bags

Give your guests the celebrity treatment with these swanky take-homes. Make a ribbon leaf set, flower, and a yarn pom-pom center for each and tack them to silk bags to match your friends' favorite colors.

For each leaf set, cut three 8" ribbon pieces. Begin with each ribbon wrong side up. Fold one end down at the middle, making a 90° angle. Fold the other end on top, matching the ends (your fold will be pointy). Gather and tack the ribbon a few inches below the point; then, trim the ribbon ends.

For each 3½" dia. flower, cut a 12" ribbon length. Pull both ends of the wire on one long ribbon edge to gather it into a tight circle; twist the wire together and trim the ends. Fold the ribbon ends under; overlap and glue them together. Follow *Pom-poms* (page 109) and wrap the yarn around the cardboard about 75 times to make each pom-pom. Trim and shape the ends to make a 2½" dia. flower center.

Sew the pieces together and add a flower to each bag. Place a gift inside to make your evening together even more memorable.

✳ 1½" wide satin ribbon for the leaves ✳ 1½" wide iridescent wire-edged ribbon for the flowers ✳ Fabric glue
✳ Novelty yarn for the flower centers ✳ 2" cardboard square ✳ 9" x 5" silk evening bags in different colors

come to the
table

Draw your guests to the table with cozy place settings. First make napkins, place mats, a table runner, or tablecloth with colorful fabric that coordinates with your dishes. They're simple to finish—just fray the edges, sew a quick hem, or use hem tape.

Instead of a large centerpiece, place a more intimate ornament "vase" on a napkin ring at each place setting. Dress up the ornaments with rub-ons (or hand paint them if that's your thing) and remove the hangers. Then, just add water and a few blooms.

Place an accordion-folded napkin on each plate and top it with an individual place card ornament decorated with Christmas wishes, your guest's name, or a simple design. Ours began as a 4" square cut from foam core. We painted it, then added rub-ons (rubber stamps work well, too) and used colored pencils to pull out design elements. Next, we tied it up with ribbon, wire, and beaded trim, and covered the knot with the brad.

✳ Ball ornaments ✳ Napkin rings ✳ Rub-on designs
or acrylic paints and paintbrushes ✳ Fresh flowers

✳ Napkins ✳ Foam core ✳ Acrylic paints and paintbrushes
✳ Rub-on designs ✳ Colored pencils ✳ Wire-edged ribbon
✳ Copper wire ✳ Beaded trim ✳ Decorative brads

entertaining
runner

When you make this table runner, the party will be at your house—even before anyone arrives. Using pieces you've felted and cut from old wool sweaters, follow your instincts to make the runner whatever shape you want, as long or short as you wish. Embellish it or keep it simple. It's all up to you.

See *Felting Wool* (page 109) to felt the sweaters. Cut random shapes from the felted wool and hand-dyed felt. Arrange the pieces, overlap the edges, and zigzag them together.

Here are some embellishing ideas to get you going. Cover some of the seams with yarn or trim. Cut felted balls in half and glue them to the runner. Sew on sequins with beaded centers. Cut strips from a sweater cuff and curl them up. Add a handful of metallic thread to the curls and sew across them, catching the thread as you go. Free expression is what it's all about.

✳ Old wool sweaters (at least 60% wool content works best) ✳ Hand-dyed felt ✳ Variegated yarn ✳ Metallic braided trim ✳ Felted wool balls ✳ Fabric glue ✳ Sequins and seed beads ✳ Metallic threads

the ties
that bind

Whether you've cooked or catered, welcome your friends wearing this fabulous apron made from scratch (it only takes a little fabric to make a great impression).

Match right sides and long edges and fold a 31" wide x 33" high fabric piece in half. For the armholes, mark $9^{1}/4$" from the top corner opposite the fold on the side and top edges. Use a large plate or mixing bowl to draw a curved line between the marks. Cut away the armholes and unfold the apron. Following the curve of the armholes, cut two 3" wide casing pieces from solid fabric. Press each short end 1" to the wrong side.

Press the straight edges of the apron piece under $^{3}/8$", then $^{5}/8$" and topstitch. Match right sides and use a $^{1}/4$" seam allowance to sew each casing to the apron along the short curved edge of the casing. Clip the curves to make the casing lie flat; then, press the casing to the back of the apron and press the remaining curved edge $^{1}/4$" to the wrong side. Refer to the *drawing* and topstitch along each curved edge of the casing, leaving the ends open for the tie.

Cut four $1^{1}/2$" x 26" solid fabric strips and use a $^{1}/4$" seam allowance to sew them together to make a $102^{1}/2$" long tie. Press each edge of the tie $^{1}/4$" to the wrong side. Match the wrong sides and long edges and press the tie in half. Topstitch along each edge of the tie. Thread each end through an armhole casing and sew jingle bells to the ends.

 1 yard of print fabric ✳ $^{1}/2$ yard of solid fabric ✳ Jingle bells

easy
elegance

Simple, yet stunning—your friends will be impressed that you arranged these yourself. First, cut the ribbon long enough to go around the vase 7 times. Start with the middle of the ribbon at the top back of the vase. Wrap it around the vase, cross and twist the ribbon, and wrap it to the back. Continue wrapping to the bottom and knot the ribbon ends at the back.

Fill 1/3 of the vase with water and mix in the flower food. Remove the thorns and greenery from the roses and berry stems; then, measure from the tops of the flowers to cut each rose the same length. Place one rose at a time in the vase, making four rows of four. Border the roses with the berry stems. Use the funnel to fill the vase with water.

✳ Ribbon (pick one that's pretty on both sides) ✳ Tall four-sided glass vase (ours has a 4" square opening and is 13" tall) ✳ Fresh flower food packet ✳ 16 white long-stem rosebuds ✳ Red coffee berries ✳ Funnel

bright lights

Here is a simple way to rejuvenate pillar candles, and it's so much fun! Start with a paper napkin that has a pattern you like. Cut it to fit the height of one of your candles. Pull the paper layers apart and wrap the patterned piece around the candle. (If one napkin isn't large enough, use two and overlap the edges a bit.) Use the hair dryer set on hot or a heat gun if you have one and slowly move the dryer up and down along one section of the candle. You'll be able to see the paper absorb the melting wax as the candle and paper meld. If your candle begins to drip, let it cool for two seconds and roll the candle over a flat surface to press out the drips—works great! (You might want to experiment with a small candle until you're able to control the melting wax and drips.) Continue with a section at a time until the napkin ends overlap. Tie a ribbon around the candle and add highlights with sequins and sequin pins. Enjoy your lit candles, but don't leave them unattended.

Never have enough candleholders? Make a bunch in no time (and on an artist's budget) from leftover ceramic tiles using glass or ceramic spray paint in bold accent colors. Work in a well-ventilated space and apply sealer to make them last.

what ties between
For a festive twist on twinkle lights, tie bright ribbon strips between the bulbs. Great way to use up ribbon scraps! Just remember, always pull the plug on unattended twinkle lights.

✳ Patterned paper napkins ✳ Pillar candles ✳ Hair dryer or heat gun ✳ Ribbon ✳ Sequins
✳ Sequin pins ✳ Ceramic tiles ✳ Spray paint for glass or ceramics ✳ Clear acrylic matte spray sealer

home

The image of a door at the end of each day's path, an entryway to the rooms where we feel most comfortable. Whether the rooms in your home are boisterous or quiet, intimate or crowded, fancy or plain—you'll find ideas in this chapter to bring the celebration home and set the stage for making merry.

Make a holiday pillow from an old sweater or wrap canvas packages with paint and polka dots. Nestle little treasures in unexpected spots. Make a holiday wreath unlike any you've ever seen before. Try our projects exactly as they're written, or change them to suit your whim—because we believe that the more you express your creative personality in your home, the more you will inspire everyone who visits you there.

one forest
five trees

What happens when you ask each of our designers to make an 18" square Christmas tree pillow? They have a great time turning their imaginings into reality, and no two pillows are alike! Turn the page for the real story on each designer's pillow, and see *About Pillows* on page 108 for the basics. Enough said; it's time to cut loose and discover your own inner tree.

kelly branches out

Kelly loved the striped pillow front fabric. She pulled together some trims and this whimsical tree appeared.

Pin velvet ribbon branches on the pillow front and drape them with a fiber garland. Zigzag the branches in place with clear nylon thread and spot glue the garland. Add a felt star and package trimmed with a satin bow.

✳ ¹/₂" wide velvet ribbon ✳ 19" square of striped fabric for the pillow front ✳ Fiber garland ✳ Clear nylon thread ✳ Fabric glue ✳ Felt scraps ✳ Satin ribbon ✳ 11" x 19" and 13" x 19" piece of velveteen for the back ✳ 18" square pillow form

kim's evergreen sweater

Kim was inspired by the return of vintage-look clothing and fabrics. She loved the idea of reusing her old sweater instead of throwing it away.

First, find that old sweater. Next, cut a 14" square from the printed felt and use scalloped scissors to cut a slightly larger solid felt square. Blanket stitch them together—see *Stitches* (page 108). Enlarge the pattern (page 119) to 263%, cut out the tree, and pin it to the front of your sweater. Machine zigzag beside the pattern edges. Cut ¹/₄" outside the stitching and whipstitch the tree onto the felt squares. Sew sequins on the tree and fabric glue the design to the pillow front.

✳ Old sweater ✳ Printed and solid felt ✳ Scallop-edged scissors ✳ Embroidery floss ✳ Sequins ✳ Fabric glue ✳ 19" square of vintage-look fabric for the pillow front and an 11" x 19" and a 13" x 19" piece for the back ✳ 18" square pillow form

lori's pom-poms

Lori wanted to use fabrics you wouldn't expect to see on a Christmas project—and making covered button ornaments was the way to go! She also liked the surprise element of just a few pom-poms on the top and bottom edges.

Fuse the triangle to the pillow front, zigzag the edges, and sew on the covered buttons (follow manufacturer's directions to cover the buttons). Complete the pillow and add *Pom-poms* (page 109) just for fun.

✳ Paper-backed fusible web ✳ Fabric triangle for the tree (Lori's is 16" tall with a 10" wide base) ✳ 19" square of corduroy fabric for the pillow front and an 11" x 19" and a 13" x 19" piece for the back ✳ Fabric scraps ✳ Button cover kits ✳ 18" square pillow form ✳ Yarn

becky's scrunchy tree

Inspired by the creative flow of ideas among friends, Becky heartily recommends working with others. In this technique, she machine stitched puckers in shimmery fabric on purpose.

To prepare the tree fabric, first stack and pin the green metallic fabric on the two muslin squares. Sew all over the pieces, slightly scrunching the fabric here and there as you go to create a textured, quilted look.

Enlarge the pattern (page 118) to 232% or make your own. Cut the tree from the scrunched fabric and zigzag it to the pillow front. Trim the tree (Becky zigzagged felt circles and tacked large sequins to hers).

✳ 19" square of green metallic fabric for the tree ✳ Two 19" squares of muslin ✳ 19" square of paisley fabric for the pillow front and an 11" x 19" and a 13" x 19" piece for the back ✳ Felt scraps ✳ Paillette sequins ✳ 18" square pillow form

anne's improv

Anne spotted a bunch of felt pieces in her crafting stash and came up with the idea to stack felt triangles into a tree shape. The trims were some she had on hand as well—wonderfully spontaneous.

Cut erratic triangles from felt and zigzag them to the pillow front to fashion your tree. For trimming, add tassels, felt circles, fabric scraps, and beads. Turn to *Stitches* (page 108) to add spiraling couching and running stitches. Add a tree skirt and topper to complete the pillow front (Anne used *Bradded Circles* from page 109 to make hers). After you construct the pillow, add the edging (*Loopy Edging* is on page 109).

✳ Felt pieces for the tree ✳ Clear nylon thread ✳ 19" square of wool felt for the pillow front and an 11" x 19" and a 13" x 19" piece for the back ✳ Tassel trim ✳ Fabric scraps ✳ Beads ✳ Embroidery floss ✳ Gold brads ✳ Fabric glue ✳ 12" x 24" wool felt for the edging ✳ 18" square pillow form

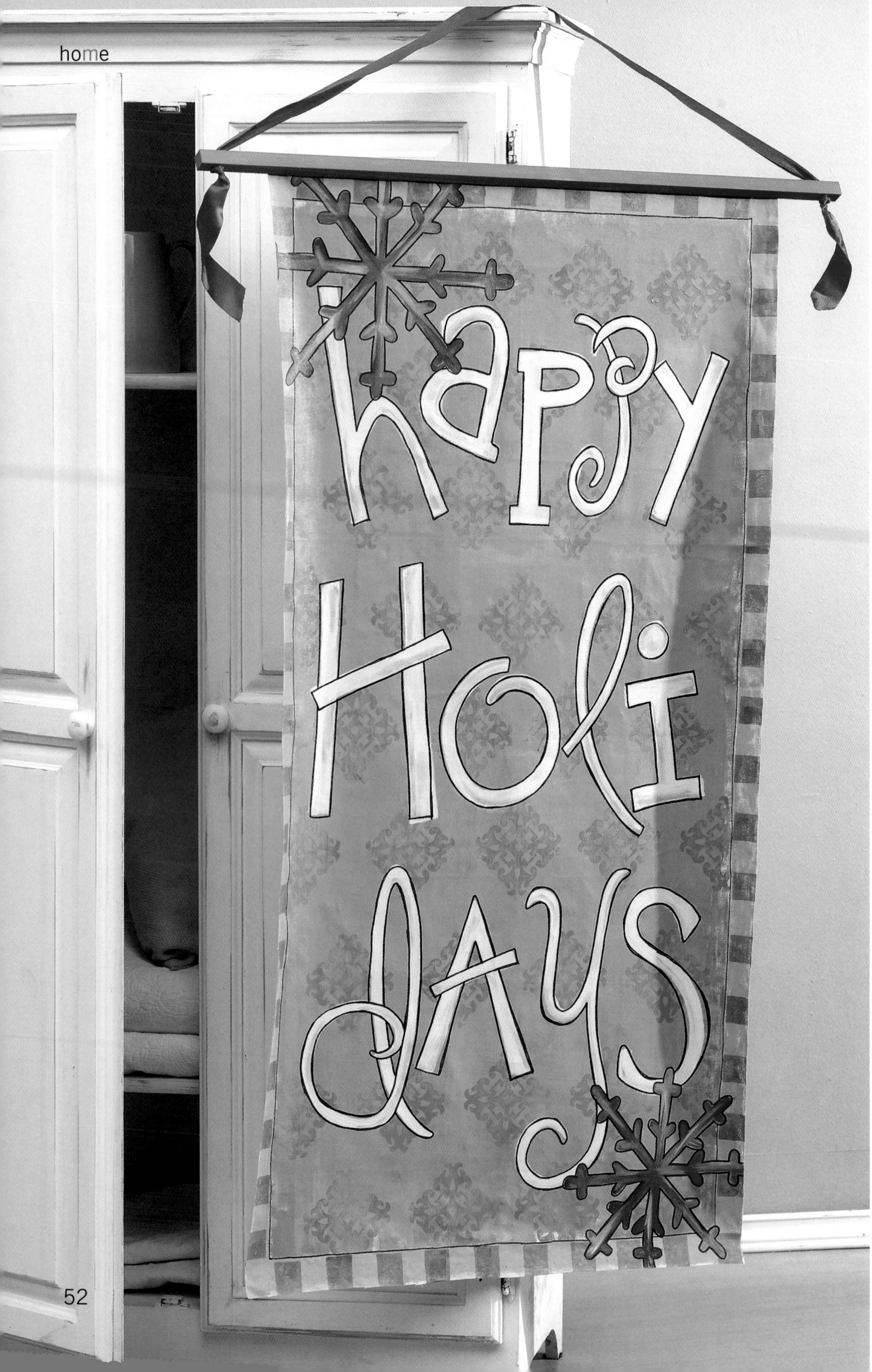
happy
Holi
days

bring on the
holidays!

Cut the canvas as large as you want it and paint the background color (just give it one coat—if you try to make it perfect, it won't look as good). Paint a border and stamp it with contrasting squares; then, add a subtle design to the background with the patterned stamp—you may want to stamp on paper, then on the canvas to cut the intensity of the paint color. Freehand your message and the snowflakes, or enlarge and transfer a computer font and the snowflake pattern (page 119). Paint the letters and snowflakes. (We used cream for the letters and blended in light gold and a soft brown while wet to shade. Using the same technique, paint the snowflakes in brighter colors.) Outline with the marker to define the design elements.

To hang the banner, drill holes through the ends of the rod and attach the ribbon. Then, staple the top of the canvas to the rod. To keep the banner from curling, glue the yardstick to the back bottom edge. Take the banner outside and spray it with sealer.

✳ Pre-gessoed artist's canvas ✳ Acrylic paints and paintbrushes ✳ Square and patterned stamps ✳ Grapite transfer paper (optional) ✳ Permanent marker (we used brown) ✳ Drill and bits ✳ Painted wooden rod ✳ Satin ribbon ✳ Staple gun ✳ Craft glue ✳ Yardstick ✳ Clear acrylic matte spray sealer

pile-up the
packages

Get your mantel in the mood with these *chic cadeaux*. Pick out several energetic paint colors and gather different sizes of artist's canvases. Paint the backgrounds, add dots (or not), and finish with ribbons and bows in colors that pop. We gave our painted presents the once-over with sandpaper for a well-traveled look.

For a quick change-of-mood in the post-season, cover the canvases with print fabrics (just staple them to the back). Next December, you'll get to "unwrap" these presents early to set the holidays in motion.

✳ Acrylic paints and paintbrushes ✳ Pre-stretched artist's canvases
✳ Coarse sandpaper

We turned a smaller version of the wreath into a cardholder by attaching the birds to clothespins.

radical
wreath

Can't keep it in? Shout joy to your world with our not-so-heavy metal wreath. Enlarge the quarter-wreath pattern on page 118, (we used 300% to make a 44"-tall wreath) and cut four shapes from sheet metal (use protective gloves and goggles when cutting sheet metal). Arrange the pieces so they overlap and tape them together. Decoupage strips of aqua tissue paper across the wreath. Then glue lime tissue over everything, and while the tissue is damp, cut away circles with the craft knife. Wipe glue from the metal circles with a damp cloth and outline the reflecting disks with glitter glue. Trim the tissue edges after they dry. Hammer three pairs of holes through each joint and wire the metal together for a permanent hold. Do the same to wire each bell to the wreath. Sandwich the edges with foil tape and toss the gloves. For added quirkiness, top the innovative wreath with a traditional red bow.

Enlarge the bird pattern (page 111) to fit your wreath, (ours are 203%) and make a flock of foam core birds. Cover them with fabric cut 1/2" bigger than the pattern and clip the fabric at the curves so you can glue the extra to the back. Cover the back with fabric and trim the edges. Add felt wings and attach the finished tweeters with foam dots. *(Woofers not included.)*

✷ Tin snips ✷ Protective gloves and goggles ✷ Galvanized sheet metal (we used 20" wide handyman coil)
✷ Double-stick tape ✷ Strong decoupage glue and sponge paintbrush ✷ Aqua and lime tissue paper
✷ Craft knife ✷ Glitter glue ✷ Hammer and awl ✷ Medium-gauge wire ✷ 8 jingle bells (we painted ours red)
✷ Silver copper foil tape ✷ Ribbon ✷ Foam core ✷ Fabric and felt scraps ✷ Fabric glue ✷ Dimensional foam dots

lighting
the way

Add color to your walkway by day and a warm glow at night. Cut tissue paper strips and glue them around the candleholders, making different-colored stripes. Brush a few coats of glue on top of the paper and let the glue dry. Pour some glitter on a piece of foil or wax paper. Brush glue along the top edge of each candleholder. Turn it over and dip it in the glitter to add sparkle. Since these luminaries are for outdoor use, spray the candleholders with several coats of sealer in a well-ventilated area. Add the candles and brighten the path home.

✳ Tissue paper in different colors ✳ Decoupage glue and sponge paintbrush
✳ Tall glass candleholders ✳ Mica glitter ✳ Foil or wax paper ✳ Clear acrylic
matte spray sealer ✳ Votive candles

choosing
sides

Who says a wreath has to be round? Cover the front of an unpainted square frame and different-size wooden discs with green scrapbook papers and sand the edges. (You can find the discs at an arts and crafts store.) Glue the discs to the frame and add a few red disc berries. Take it outside to spray it with sealer and top it off with a sassy red bow.

✳ Craft glue ✳ Unpainted square frame ✳ Assorted wooden discs
✳ Green and red printed scrapbook papers ✳ Sandpaper
✳ Clear acrylic matte spray sealer ✳ Red ribbon

candlestick
leggings

For some off-the-cuff candlestick covers, cut the foot from each toe sock to make a tube the height of a candlestick. Cut the sock open from top to bottom, wrap it around the candlestick tightly, and pin it in place. Cut away the extra fabric. Whipstitch from top to bottom (see *Stitches*, page 108). Cut two toes from the foot and stuff each with a wooden bead. Cut a long piece of floss and sew a running stitch around the top of one bead and gather it tight; then, repeat for the other end—just don't cut the floss in the middle! Tie the floss around the candlestick (like those mittens-on-a-string for little kids). When the weather warms up, take off the socks.

✳ Striped toe socks ✳ Wooden candlesticks (we painted them in different colors)
✳ Brightly-colored embroidery floss ✳ Wooden beads

scrappy quilt

Never pieced a quilt top before? This is an easy one to start with, because you don't have to make precise cuts. Find fabrics that work well together to reflect your color scheme. Wash the fabrics separately to get any shrinking or fading out of the way and press the pieces. The fun begins on the next page.

✳ ¹/₂ yd each of four print fabrics ✳ 1 yd each of seven solids ✳ 4 yds of backing fabric ✳ Rotary cutter, ruler, and cutting mat or scissors ✳ 9" cardboard square ✳ 53" x 61" piece of low-loft batting ✳ Embroidery floss ✳ 6¹/₄ yds of double-fold bias binding

These yardages are based on fabrics with a 40" usable width and will make a 49" x 57" quilt. Match right sides and use a ¼" seam allowance unless otherwise noted.

For the quilt top, matching the selvage edges, fold each of the ½-yd and 1-yd pieces, and cut along the fold; then, cut off the selvages. Look at drawing 1 and cut each piece from edge to edge into different-width strips (about 20" long)—you don't want them to be perfect rectangles, so cut each strip a little skinnier on one end, but at least 1" wide.

Match long edges and sew random strips together till you have a 48" long striped piece. Press all the seams in one direction. Follow drawing 2, and using the cardboard square, cut six 9" squares from the piece with the stripes running diagonally (not a perfect diagonal, just slanty).

Continue sewing strips together and cutting them into squares until you have 42 squares. Arrange the squares in a pattern that you like. (This is a freeform quilt, so the stripes and points won't line up.) Use a ½" seam allowance to sew six squares together for each row; press the seams open. Sew the rows together.

To back the quilt, cut the backing into two 2-yard pieces. Trim the selvages. Sew the pieces together along the long edges, making a tube (drawing 3a). Follow drawing 3b to match the seams and press along the right fold; cut through both layers 6¾" to the right of the seam. Open up the pieced backing (drawing 3c) and trim it to 61" x 53".

drawing 1

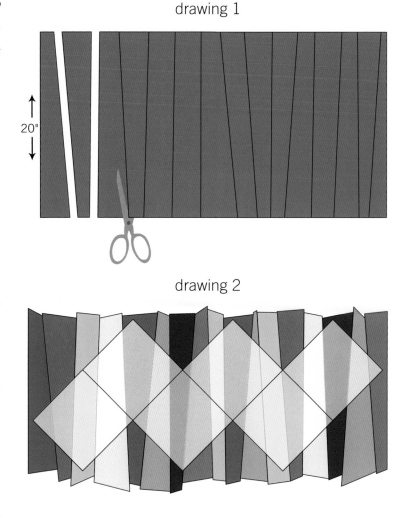

drawing 2

drawing 3a   drawing 3b   drawing 3c

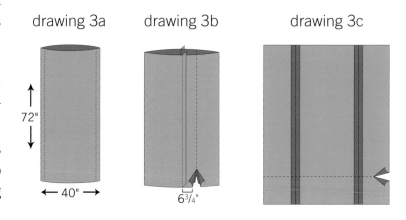

Place the backing wrong side up. Center and layer the batting and quilt top (right side up) on the backing; pin the layers together. Use two lengths of floss to sew the quilt and backing together at the intersections and tie them off. Sew the layers together $1/8$" from the edge of the quilt top. Trim the batting and backing to the same size as the quilt top.

Sandwich the edges of the quilt in the fold of the bias binding and sew the binding to the quilt, mitering at the corners.

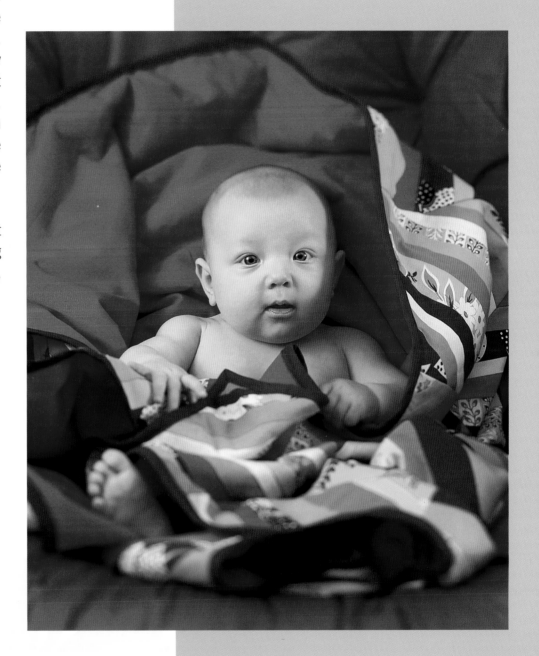

k-9
coasters

Doggy dining at its finest. After you've finished with a sheet of corkboard and a little paint, Phydeaux will think she's in a 5-star bistro for barkers. Cut cork circles a few inches larger than the dog's dishes and paint rings around a solid circle on each. Using the pattern on page 120 (we used the pattern at full size and enlarged to 133%), cut snowflakes from a sheet of stencil plastic; then, stencil flurries around the edges of the coasters. Go outside (but leave your furry friend in) and spray the coasters with sealer to guard against stray drips or drool.

✳ Corkboard ✳ Acrylic paints and paint brushes ✳ Stencil plastic ✳ Stencil brush ✳ Clear acrylic matte spray sealer   69

gifts

Here's the good news, all wrapped up for you: Creating just one handcrafted gift this year can give you an unmatched sense of I-did-it-myself satisfaction. Anyone on your list lucky enough to receive one of your original creations will know just how important you think they are.

Each craft project in this collection is completely doable, whether you make it just as you see it, or make it entirely yours. So instead of fighting the shopping hordes, you can get lost in the creative flow.

The perfect holiday gift—every store claims to have it. This year, you can be the one who's giving it.

what's outside
the box?

We asked each of our designers to turn a simple wooden box into a meaningful gift—and did they ever! The basics are easy, and whether you are a paint-color purist or like to blend and shade, we believe one of these boxes will unleash your creative spirit. Here's an overview; for more details and close-ups, look at pages 74 through 77.

Get started by removing the latch hardware from a wooden box. If you won't be reusing the latch, fill the holes with putty. Glue wood trim or feet on the box if you like. Sand the box and wipe it with a tack cloth to remove the dust. Basecoat with acrylic paint. Transfer one of our patterns (beginning on page 120) or make your own. Next, paint the design and seal it in a well-ventilated space. Add hardware, knobs, or line the inside. Take our ideas and run—your box will be a one-of-a-kind delight.

✳ 8¹⁄₂"w x 5¹⁄₄"d x 3¹⁄₂"h wooden box ✳ Wood putty and wood glue (optional) ✳ Sandpaper ✳ Tack cloth ✳ Acrylic paints and paintbrushes ✳ Graphite transfer paper (optional) ✳ Clear acrylic matte spray sealer ✳ Additional supplies are listed with the individual projects.

really wild flowers

Lori experimented with lots of color on her box. She enjoys turning designs from nature into simple graphic patterns.

Cut the wood trim to fit, mitering at the corners. Glue the trim to the prepared box. Fill in the corners and the hardware holes with putty. Drill holes for the wood knob, the elastic closure, and the button knob. Basecoat the wood knob and box inside and out with black. Paint the box sides and trim (Lori suggests leaving the brushstrokes showing). Paint the background on the lid and wood knob. Enlarge the patterns (page 122) to 108% and transfer them to the lid and wood knob. Paint the design and add any shading or highlights. Attach the wood knob to the lid. Apply sealer. Thread a knotted elastic loop through the top hole on the front. Run another elastic piece through the button shank and the box; tie a knot.

✳ Handsaw ✳ Decorative wood trim ✳ Wood glue ✳ Wood putty ✳ Drill and bit ✳ 2" dia. wood knob ✳ Graphite transfer paper ✳ Black elastic cord ✳ ⅞" dia. black button

st. nick's wish box

Anne knew she wanted to make a wish box after looking at her son's list for Santa Claus. He collects nutcrackers and their simple features were an inspiration for St. Nick's face.

Glue wood knobs to the bottom of the prepared box. Cut the trim to fit, mitering at the corners. Glue and nail the trim to the lid and box. Fill in the corners and nail holes with putty. Basecoat the box inside and out. Enlarge the patterns (page 124) to 108% and transfer them to the box. Paint the designs and add details with the pen. Sand the box lightly and apply sealer. Line the inside lid and bottom of the box with fabric (Anne used sweater pieces left over from other projects for a warm and wooly lining). Finish it off with yarn glued around the fabric edges.

✳ Wood glue ✳ Four wood knobs for feet
✳ Handsaw ✳ Decorative wood trim
✳ Small trim nails and tack hammer
✳ Wood putty ✳ Graphite transfer paper
✳ Black fine-point permanent pen ✳ Fabric glue ✳ Soft, thick fabrics ✳ Variegated yarn

triple play

Paint, flocking, and copper—Kim challenged her inner artist with this unusual combination of crafting techniques.

Enlarge the patterns (page 123) to 120% and cut, from copper tooling foil, four corner pieces, one front and two side rectangles, and an oval slightly larger than the dotted oval design. Tape the dotted patterns over the copper pieces and hammer the pattern onto the copper to make an impression. (Practice on a scrap piece of tooling foil to get the hang of how hard to tap the awl for the look you want. The dots are only a guide—no need to try to hit every one).

Basecoat the prepared box. Draw your own design or transfer the solid black lines from the enlarged pattern onto the top of the box. Center and draw around the front and side copper rectangles to mark their placement. Paint the design on the top and add borders, if you like, around the marked areas on the front and sides. Seal the box.

Follow the manufacturer's directions to flock the painted design. Tape; then, tack the copper pieces to the box. Bend each copper corner as shown in blue on the pattern and tack it to the box, overlapping the shaded area of the pattern on the side of the box. Reattach the latch hardware (Kim spray painted hers to match the copper tooling).

✳ Tin snips ✳ 36-gauge copper tooling foil ✳ Transparent tape
✳ Hammer and awl ✳ Graphite transfer paper ✳ Flocking kit (ours includes flocking adhesive and fibers) ✳ Copper-colored tacks ✳ Metallic copper spray paint (use in a well-ventilated area)

audrey's crayons
Kelly was given the idea for a chalkboard motif when she caught sight of her daughter's crayon box.

Prepare the box, adding beads for the feet, and basecoat with light green. Measure and mark the placement for the chalkboard and stripes. Draw triangles in the corners to continue the stripes onto the lid (the seamstress in Kelly comes out with this mitered look). Leaving the chalkboard area unpainted, paint the rest of the box and allow to dry. Scuff up the paint with sandpaper and seal the box. Paint the chalkboard and follow manufacturer's directions for curing and writing on the board. Reattach the latch hardware to the box.

✳ Wood glue ✳ 1" dia. wood beads (Kelly found beads with a flat side) ✳ Chalkboard paint

peace on earth
Becky has long admired a collection of wood-burned boxes and thought it would be fun to complement the technique with paint. Her cat modeled for her and with the help of an imagined bluebird, her box is all about peaceful coexistence.

Glue the plaque to the bottom of the box. Fill in the latch hardware holes with putty and sand the box. Enlarge the designs (pages 120 to 122) to 126% and transfer them onto the sides and lid (Becky added the heart and leaf design to the inside bottom of her box). Follow manufacturer's directions to outline the designs with the wood burning tool (first practice on scrap wood, using different sides of the tips to make dots and lines with varied thicknesses). Thin paint with water so the wood grain will show through and paint the box. Seal the box inside and out.

✳ Wood glue ✳ 6½" x 9½" wooden plaque ✳ Wood putty ✳ Graphite transfer paper ✳ Wood burning tool with assorted tips

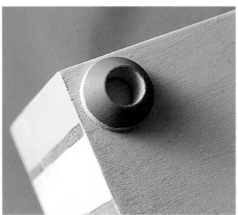
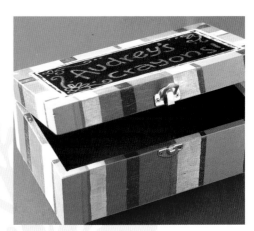

painted
postcard

It's amazing what you can mail these days—send a holiday postcard you painted yourself! Draw your own design or enlarge the pattern (page 125) to 117% and transfer it onto the canvas board. (We've given you the whole flower—position it however you like.) Lightly erase the transferred lines so you can barely see them. Paint the design. (If you want to paint the design the way we did, number your paints according to the key on the pattern, then paint.) After the paint dries, apply several coats of sealer for safe traveling. Glue cardstock on the back. Address the card, write a message, and add postage.

✳ Graphite transfer paper ✳ 5" x 7" canvas board ✳ Acrylic paints and paintbrushes (we used three red-to-pink shades, three gold shades, and one green) ✳ Clear matte acrylic sealer ✳ Craft glue ✳ Textured cardstock

artistic
license

Put on your work gloves and goggles and cut up license plates to make a simple design. (To change a plate color, just turn it over for silver, or use metal paint to get the look you want. Touch up numbers or letters with a paint pen.) Arrange the pieces on the board and draw a background. Remove the pieces and paint the background with bold brush strokes (we added shading and highlights while the paints were wet to give the background some movement). Nail the plate pieces to the board and attach the hanger on the back.

floppable geoffrey

They seemed like such a good idea at the time, didn't they? Well, dig out your just-like-new toe socks from the back of the drawer and turn them into a Geoffrey pal for someone you love. It's like giving a non-stop hug—what a fabulous idea!

✳ Two knee-high pairs of toe socks for the arms and legs ✳ Knee-high striped sock for the body ✳ Sock with a solid-color toe for the head ✳ Doll stuffing pellets (or use lentils if giving to a small child) ✳ Polyester fiberfill ✳ Yarn for the hair ✳ 2¹⁄₂" cardboard square ✳ Felt scraps for the face ✳ Fabric glue

drawing 1

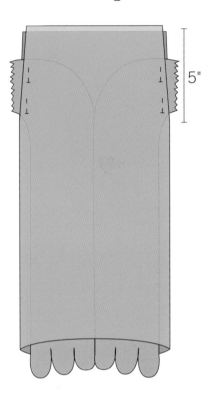

Match right sides and use a ¹/₄" seam allowance unless otherwise noted.

For the arms and legs, cut each toe sock along the length of the sock so it's three toes wide at the bottom and a little narrower at the top. Sew the long side up and turn it right side out. Pour pellets or lentils into the toes/fingers and finish stuffing with fiberfill.

Cut the foot and cuff from the body sock, leaving a tube about 12" long. Turn the sock wrong side out and lay it flat. Follow _drawing 1_ and make a 5"-long tapered cut on opposite sides for the arm openings and neck. Put the arms inside the tube, pinning the open end of each arm at the bottom of each cut. Sew up the tapered cuts and turn the body right side out.

Turn the bottom of the body under ¹/₄", insert the tops of the legs, and pin. Sew across the end. Stuff the body with about an inch of pellets or lentils and fill it with fiberfill. For the hair, see _Pom-poms_ (page 109) and wrap yarn around the cardboard square and tie off, but don't cut the loops. Slide the yarn off the square and fan out the hair. Turn the neck opening under ¹/₂", tuck the tied end of the hair into the opening, and sew the neck closed. (Sounds kind of weird, but trust us, it works.)

Make each ear by stitching together two U shapes from sock scraps (ours are 3" tall). Turn them right side out and stuff them with fiberfill; turn the open ends under ¹/₂". Cut across the sock for the head just below the heel and toss the top. Stuff the head with fiberfill and turn the open end under ¹/₂". Match the folded ends and sew the ears to the top of the head. Overlapping the ends about ¹/₂", follow _drawing 2_ to hand sew the head to the body. Cut nose and eye pieces from felt and glue them to the face. If you'd like, clip some of the yarn hair loops for bangs.

drawing 2

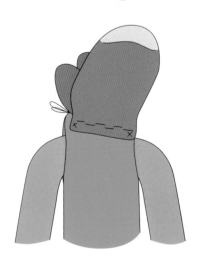

it's about
time

Make time—for real. Drill a hole through the center of the plate for the clock shaft. Prime, then lightly sand the plate and wipe it with the tack cloth. Enlarge our pattern (page 125) to 105% and transfer it onto the front of the plate, or draw your own design. Paint the plate, then lightly sand it after it's dry. Sand the spots at each quarter hour where the wood balls will be glued. Paint the round part of the wood balls and glue the flat sides to the plate. Paint the numbers and varnish the clock.

Paint the hands, if you'd like, and add the clock movement. Coil one end of each rod, leaving 3" of the other end straight. Staple the straight ends to the back of the clock.

✳ Drill and bit ✳ 8½" dia. wood plate ✳ Primer ✳ Paintbrushes ✳ Sandpaper and tack cloth
✳ Graphite transfer paper (optional) ✳ Acrylic paints ✳ Four 1¼" doll head wood balls ✳ Wood glue
✳ Satin varnish ✳ Clock movement to fit the thickness of the plate (remember the battery!)
✳ Eight 12" long soft metal rods (available at craft stores) ✳ Staple gun

sweater
afghan

Browse the back of the closet, resale shops, and yard sales, and you'll find enough sweaters to make even the largest afghan for chilly evenings. Cut squares and rectangles from old sweaters and arrange them in rows. Zigzag the pieces together for one row at a time; then, zigzag the rows together. Cut a piece of backing fabric $1^1/2$" larger than the afghan on all sides. Match wrong sides and center the afghan on the backing. Fold one edge of the backing $1/2$" to the wrong side; fold again over the front of the afghan and zigzag. Finish the other three sides the same way.

Use yarn to tack the afghan and backing together at intersections of the sweater pieces, add buttons, and tie them off. *Warning: If word gets out to your friends that you made this afghan, you'll have a new part-time job.*

✳ Assorted old sweaters ✳ Backing fabric ✳ Yarn ✳ Buttons

treats

Now, art may be food for the soul, but only edibles can please the palate. Bon-bons, rock candy, and five of our designers' favorite easy recipes answer that need nicely. We even show you how to wrap and package the treats in ways to satisfy hungry eyes.

This chapter is dedicated to that one-of-a-kind gift you've always heard about. No size charts or wish lists required.

All you have to do is find the kitchen and get gifty.

bon-bon
box

There's more than one surprise inside this box—as the candy disappears, the recipe is revealed. Make two copies of the chocolate bon-bon recipe collage on cardstock (or use different fonts to make a collage of your own candy recipe). Line the inside of the box with the collage cardstock; then, tape acetate inside the lid. Cover the outside of the box with scrapbook papers and the corners with white or colored tape. Fill the box with candy. Make a tag and tie a ribbon around the box to keep it safe until it gets where it's going.

※ 6¹/₄" square box with lid cutout (we found ours at a scrapbook store)
※ Chocolate bon-bons (recipe on page 126) or a favorite home-made candy
※ 12" x 12" white cardstock ※ Craft glue ※ Double-sided tape ※ Clear acetate sheet
※ Scrapbook papers ※ White or colored tape ※ Hole punch ※ Ribbon

rockin' candy
cones

Who'd believe these began as rustic flower holders? Tear paper pieces and randomly glue them on the inside and outside of each cone. Hot glue tinsel around the top of the cone and make an oval on the front. Add a rub-on to the center of the oval. Our cones came with star charms, so we glittered them. Instead of filling the cones with flowers, make them blossom with a bouquet of rock candy—sweet!

❋ Metal cones (found with garden supplies) ❋ Scrapbook paper ❋ Craft glue
❋ Hot glue gun ❋ Tinsel trim ❋ Rub-on initials ❋ Glitter ❋ Rock candy swizzle sticks

double dipping
allowed

To make this striking candy jar, color copy the tag (page 127) onto cardstock and cut it out. Wrap ribbon around the jar and attach the tag to the ribbon with the brad.

Double-Dipped Cranberries
Follow package directions to melt white candy coating and drop in a few fresh cranberries at a time. Scoop them out onto wax paper to harden. Dip the berries a second time to make them especially good. Pour the hardened candy into the jar along with some fresh berries for color.

✳ Glass jar ✳ White cardstock ✳ Red velvet ribbon ✳ Silver brad

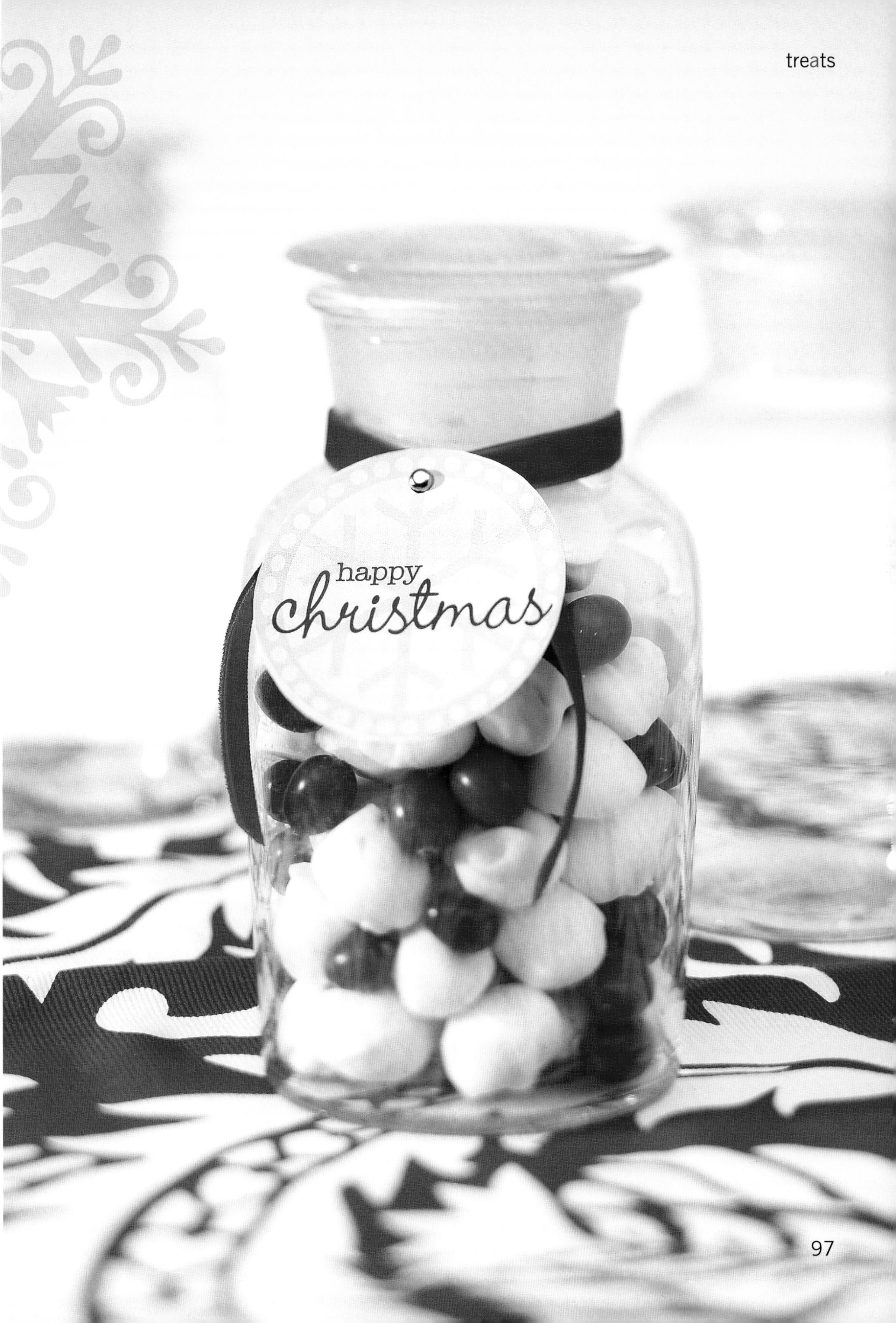
happy
christmas

happy
holidays
from Becky

stick
shift

Gear up for gift-giving with this pretzel-filled canister. For the lid, glue a cardstock circle the size of the canister opening to the back of the lined paper. Cut the paper ½" larger than the cardstock, clip the edges, and fold down the sides. Glue a scalloped paper band around the sides of the lid. Make a layered cardstock tag and add a message with rub-ons. Hot glue a button to the tag and the tag to the lid.

Using the pattern (page 119), cut a fan from scrapbook paper. Glue a piece of trim cut from the doily to the round edge and fold the fan. Glue paper strips across the bottom of the fan to hold its shape. Decorate the fan (we used a chenille stem, button, sequin, and pearls) and glue a ribbon hanger to the back.

Chocolate-Caramel Pretzel Sticks
20 caramels
1 T. milk
9 pretzel sticks
Chocolate and white candy coating
Chopped nuts, crushed peppermint candy, sprinkles

For the best of sweet and salty, place the unwrapped caramels and milk in an 8 oz. glass measuring cup and melt in the microwave on high for 30-45 seconds, or until the mixture starts to bubble. Stir until smooth and let cool slightly. Dip pretzels in the caramel about halfway up the stick. Let the excess drip, then place them in short juice glasses, dipped end up (be careful not to let the pretzels touch each other). Let the caramel set up to a firm consistency (about 10 minutes).

Place two blocks of chocolate candy coating in a glass bowl and melt in the microwave for 30 seconds; stir. Heat for 30 more seconds and stir. Spoon chocolate onto the coated pretzels, covering the caramel; let the excess drip into the bowl and place the pretzels in the glasses. When slightly cool, roll them in nuts, crushed peppermints, or sprinkles. Or, melt white candy coating and spoon it into a plastic bag. Cut off a corner and drizzle it over the chocolate.

✳ Glass canister without lid (ours is 10" tall with a 3½" dia.) ✳ Craft glue ✳ Cardstock
✳ Lined paper ✳ Scallop-edged scissors ✳ Scrapbook papers ✳ Rub-on letters ✳ Hot glue gun
✳ Buttons ✳ Tracing paper ✳ 5" dia. doily ✳ Items to decorate fan ✳ Ribbon

pizzelles' box

Untie this box, and you'll unleash goodness. Cover the box with striped paper and line it with cardstock. Add shredded paper and pizzelles to the box. To make the wrap, overlap the ends of two cardstock pieces by $1/2$" and glue them together. Follow *Making Patterns* (page 109) and trace a whole pattern (page 127) onto tracing paper. Enlarge the traced pattern to 118%, center it over the seam of the cardstock, and cut out the wrap. Glue the flaps (colored gray on the pattern) to the inside of the wrap. Fold along the remaining dotted lines and glue the corner triangles (colored blue) to the side flaps. Glue ribbon along the top edges. Fold the wrap around the box, tie it up with a ribbon, and tie on a coordinating tag.

Pizzelles
$3/4$ c. sugar
3 eggs
$1/2$ c. butter, melted and cooled
1 t. vanilla extract
$3/4$ t. anise extract
$13/4$ c. flour
2 t. baking powder
Powdered sugar

Beat sugar and eggs. Add the butter and extracts. Sift flour and baking powder together and stir into egg mixture. Drop a spoonful of batter onto a pizzelle maker at the back of each motif (our motifs have a 3" dia.). Close the maker and cook for 30-45 seconds. Remove from the maker with a small spatula and trim around each cookie with kitchen scissors. Sprinkle with powdered sugar. Makes 30 pizzelles.

✳ $41/2$" square x $23/4$" high papier-mâché box without lid ✳ Craft glue ✳ Striped scrapbook paper ✳ 12" x 12" solid cardstock ✳ Shredded paper ✳ Tracing paper ✳ $3/8$" wide satin ribbon ✳ Scallop-edged scissors ✳ Rub-on initial ✳ Hole punch ✳ Embroidery floss

snack
pack

For the perfect candy clutch, make our felt bag or try your hand at a paper version. Follow the *drawing* to cut the corners from red felt. Fold the felt into a box and sew the sides together, allowing the lid flap to hang loose. Follow *Stitches* (page 108) and use floss to blanket stitch along the sides and around the flap. Glue a felt cover to the cardboard square and trim the edges; place the square in the bottom of the bag. Cut a ³/₄" x 17" strip each of green and orange felt. Loop the felt strips to make a 3¹/₂" dia. bow and sew them together at the center. Sew the button and bow to the flap. Adhere the fastener to the bag and fill it with a plastic bag of peanut clusters.

Peanut Clusters
12-oz. pkg. of semi-sweet chocolate chips
12-oz. pkg. of white candy coating
8 oz. salted Spanish peanuts

Microwave chocolate chips and candy coating in a glass bowl for 30 seconds and stir. Continue to heat and stir, just until melted. Stir in peanuts. Drop by tablespoonfuls onto wax paper and cool. Makes 48 mouth-watering candies.

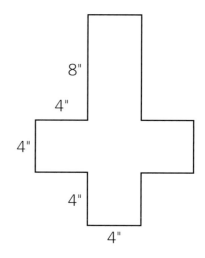

8"
4"
4"
4"
4"

✳ 12" x 16" piece of red felt ✳ Green and orange embroidery floss ✳ Fabric glue ✳ 3³/₄" cardboard square ✳ Scraps of green and orange felt ✳ Button ✳ Hook and loop fastener

cookie
accoutrements

The perfect ensemble for a budding baker! To fashion a label for the tin, cut rolled-out Paperclay with the large cookie cutter. Press alphabet stamps into the clay to add the message. Make impressions in the clay for decoration (we used the end of a paintbrush, a pen cap, and a fancy button). Use a marker cap to cut two holes in the clay for the ribbon to run through. Allow the clay to dry for a day. Lightly paint the label, and while it's wet, sprinkle it with glitter.

Use scalloped scissors to cut a folded scrapbook paper topper for the cookie mix, frosting, and sprinkle bags (next page). Punch holes through each topper and bag (above the zipper), add a stamped tag, and tie with ribbon. Cut two scalloped paper circles slightly smaller than the bottom of the tin. Place one in the tin with the recipe, mixes, sprinkles, and food coloring on top. Add the remaining circle, the cookie cutters, and the lid. Tie the label around the tin with ribbon.

✳ 8" dia. cookie tin (ours has a lid with a plastic insert) ✳ Creative Paperclay® ✳ Large cookie cutter or decorative jelly mold ✳ Alphabet stamps ✳ Marker cap ✳ Acrylic paint and sponge brush ✳ Mica glitter ✳ Scallop-edged scissors ✳ Scrapbook papers ✳ Hole punch ✳ Ink pad ✳ Tag ✳ Ribbons ✳ Red and green food coloring ✳ Cookie cutters to fit in the tin

Cookie Mix
³/₄ c. powdered sugar
1¹/₂ c. flour
¹/₂ t. baking soda
¹/₂ t. cream of tartar
¹/₂ c. butter, softened
1 c. powdered sugar
Candy sprinkles

Sift the first four ingredients together. Blend in the butter with a pastry blender. Pour the mix into a reclosable plastic bag and store in the refrigerator.
Pour 1 c. powdered sugar in another bag for the frosting mix, and pour the sprinkles in a small bag for decorating. Include the Sugar Cookie and Frosting Recipes with the mix.

Sugar Cookie Recipe
(keep cookie mix refrigerated until ready to use)
1 egg
1 t. vanilla extract
¹/₂ t. almond extract

Stir the egg and extracts into the cookie mix and blend the ingredients by hand. Cover the dough and chill. Roll the dough onto a floured surface to ¹/₄" thickness and cut out shapes. Bake at 375° on a lightly greased cookie sheet for 7 to 8 minutes or until the edges begin to brown. Cool on a wire rack. Makes 2¹/₂ to 3 dozen cookies.

Frosting
Empty the frosting bag into a bowl and add 1 T. water. Stir and add water as needed for spreading consistency. Divide the frosting into three plastic bags. Add 1 to 2 drops of food coloring to two of the bags. Snip a tiny corner from each bag to use it as a frosting tube. Frost the cookies and add sprinkles.

cookie
mix

frosting

toppings

general instructions

Stitches

Follow the drawings to bring the needle up at odd numbers and down at even numbers.

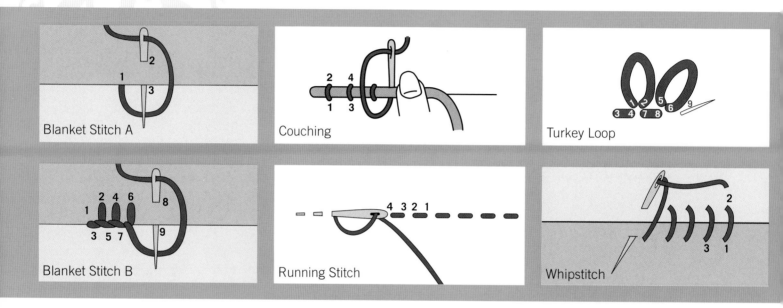

Blanket Stitch A

Couching

Turkey Loop

Blanket Stitch B

Running Stitch

Whipstitch

About Pillows

Ultra-modern, rustic, chic, or funky? Choose fabrics and trims to reflect your style and color palette. You'll need a 19" square fabric front, and for the back, cut an 11" x 19" and a 13" x 19" piece. Design your own tree or pick from our patterns on page 118 or 119. Stitch, fuse, or use fabric glue to attach your tree to the pillow front and trim the tree until you're happy in your heart. Find more ideas on pages 50 and 51.

Next, sew a 1/4" hem along one long edge of each back piece. With the hemmed edges overlapping, match right sides and sew the back pieces to the front with a 1/2" seam. Turn the pillow right side out and insert an 18" square pillow form.

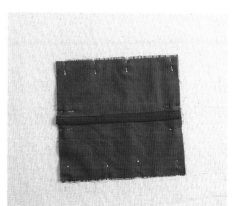

Bradded Circles

For the tree skirt on *Anne's Improv* pillow, fold ten 2½" dia. fabric circles in quarters and tack the folded points in pairs along the bottom of the tree. Then, tie the pairs together with brads that cover the points.

For the tree topper, tack four quarter-circles to the center of an unfolded circle, add a brad in the middle, and glue it to the top of the tree with fabric glue.

Loopy Edging

Sew a ¾" x 24" felt strip every ½" to the pillow edge, making loops between the stitches. Just cut more strips as you need them, until the pillow is surrounded by the loopy edging. (Or should that be edgy looping?)

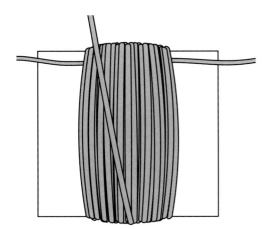

Pom-poms

Place a 6" piece of yarn along the top edge of a 2" cardboard square. Wrap yarn around and around the square and the yarn piece (the more you wrap, the fluffier the pom-pom). Tie the wound yarn together tightly with the 6" piece. Cut the loops opposite the tie; then fluff and trim the pom-pom into shape.

Making Patterns

When only half a pattern is given (shown by a solid blue line on the pattern), fold tracing paper in half. Place the fold along the blue line and trace the pattern half. Turn the tracing paper over and draw over the traced lines on the remaining side of the paper to form a whole pattern.

Felting Wool

It's fun to felt an old wool sweater. (Choose a sweater with wool content of 60% or higher to keep from having to finish the edges.) Since felting causes lots (and lots) of wool pills that could clog your drain, place the sweater in a lingerie bag or pillowcase to protect your machine. Wash and rinse in hot water on the heavy agitation and heavy soil settings. Wash it a second time for a tighter weave. Hang to dry (the amount of pilling would be too much for a dryer, even in a bag or pillowcase). When the felted sweater is dry, treat it just like felt and cut it into any shape.

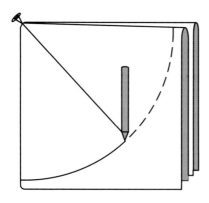

Cutting a Fabric Circle

Matching right sides, fold a fabric square in half from top to bottom and again from left to right. Tie one end of a string to a pencil. Decide the diameter you want your circle to be (including the hem if you want one). Measure half this distance along the string from the pencil. Insert a thumbtack through the string at that point and through the folded corner of the fabric. Holding the tack in place and keeping the string taut, mark the cutting line.

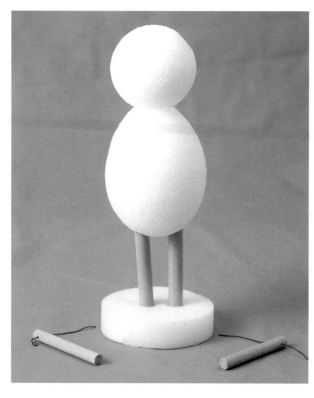

About Santa and Company

The whole crew has the same humble beginnings. To get started, cut a small notch in the foam head so it will rest on the tip of the body and glue them together. Cut 3"-long arms and 6"-long legs from the dowel. Drill a small hole though one end of each arm. Cut holes in the base for the legs and glue them in place. Insert the legs in the bottom of the body.

Cover the framework with Paperclay, dipping your finger in water and smoothing the clay as you go. Build the clay up for areas like boots, noses (or muzzles), and beards. If you like, cut a hat shape from a foam ball or fold a paper cone hat and cover it with clay. You can also make separate clay pieces (like ears and hands) and add them in while they're wet. Add clay to the arm dowels if you wish; then, allow to dry overnight. Lightly sand, then paint and watch your character come to life. Attach each arm to the body with a 4" wire length (or attach both arms with one 8"-long piece) and coil the wire ends to secure. Embellish as you please.

✳ Craft knife ✳ 3" dia. foam ball for the head and 5"-tall foam egg for the body ✳ Craft glue ✳ Handsaw ✳ ³⁄₈" dia. dowel rod ✳ Drill and bit ✳ 4" dia. x 1" thick foam base ✳ Creative Paperclay® ✳ Additional foam ball or scrapbook paper (optional) ✳ Sandpaper ✳ Acrylic paints and paintbrushes ✳ Medium-gauge wire ✳ Wire cutters ✳ Needle-nose pliers ✳ Embellishments are listed with the individual characters on pages 12 and 13.

not your typical partridge, page 14
radical wreath, page 57

snowbound chalet, page 17

not your typical partridge, page 14

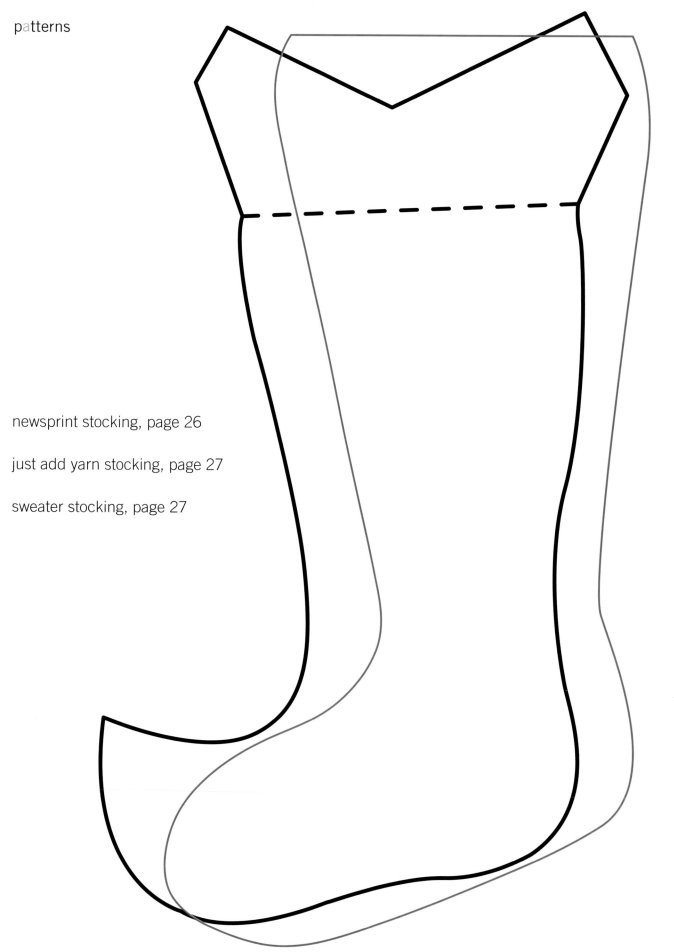

newsprint stocking, page 26

just add yarn stocking, page 27

sweater stocking, page 27

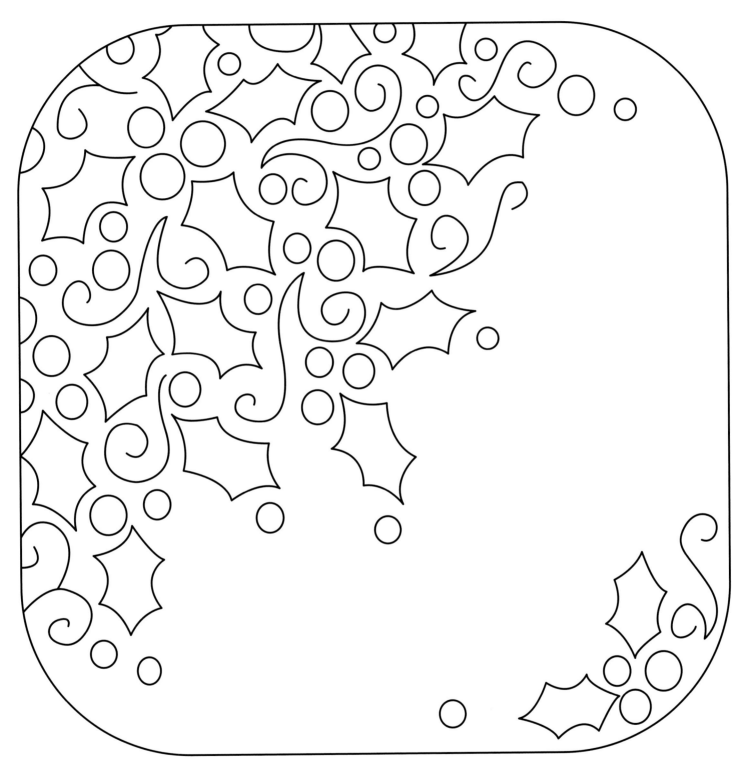

holly splash, page 33

strictly ornamental, page 33

stress-free snowman, page 32

wintry woods, page 32

by the chimney, page 33

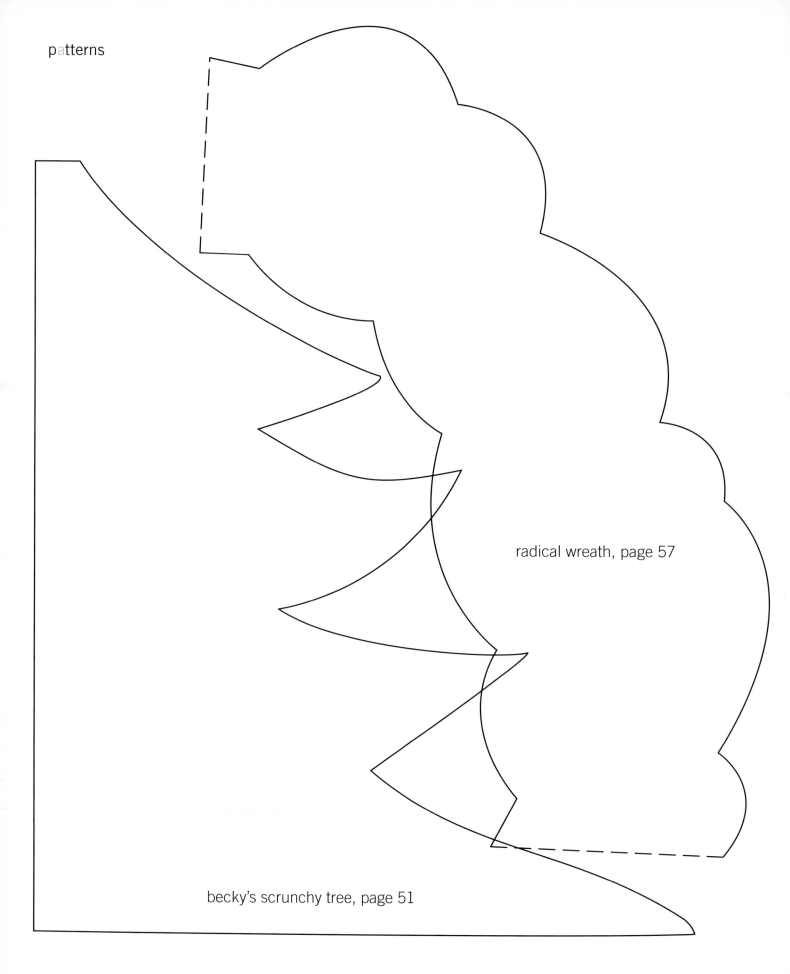

radical wreath, page 57

becky's scrunchy tree, page 51

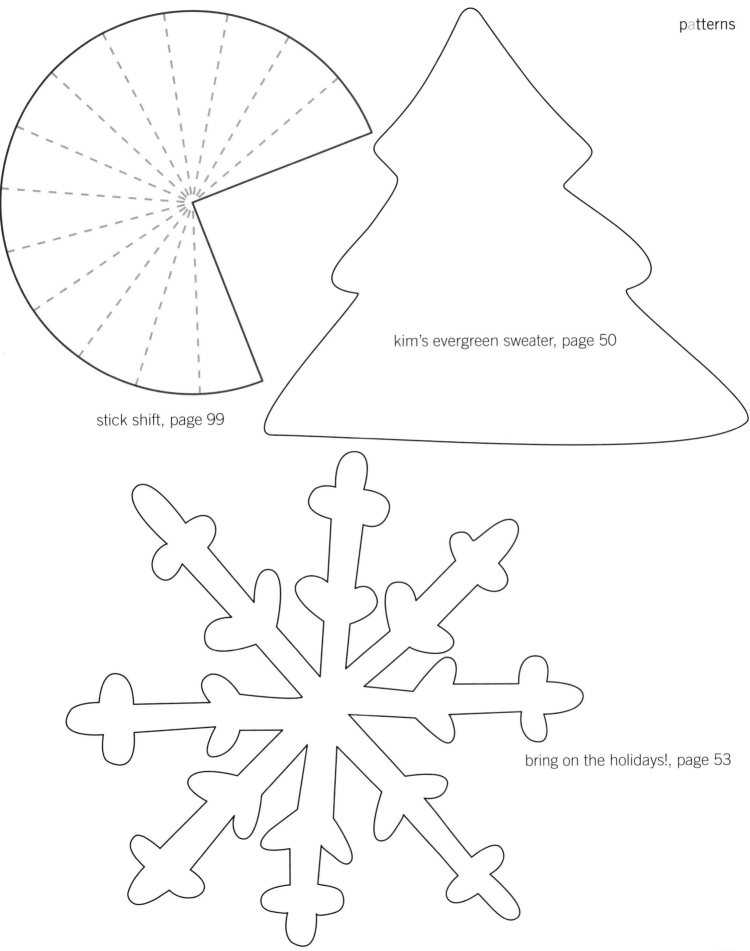

stick shift, page 99

kim's evergreen sweater, page 50

bring on the holidays!, page 53

patterns

k-9 coasters, page 69

peace on earth,
page 76

peace on earth, page 76

peace on earth, page 76

patterns

peace on earth, page 76

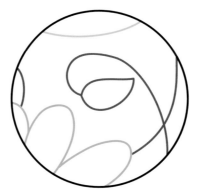

really wild flowers, page 74

corner piece

side

front

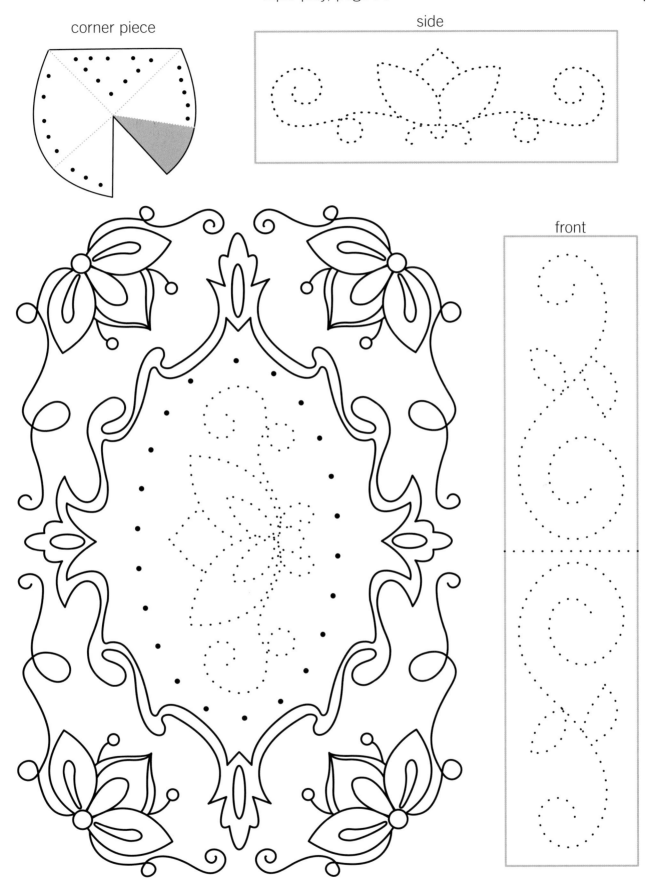

St. Nick's Wish Box

st. nick's wish box, page 75

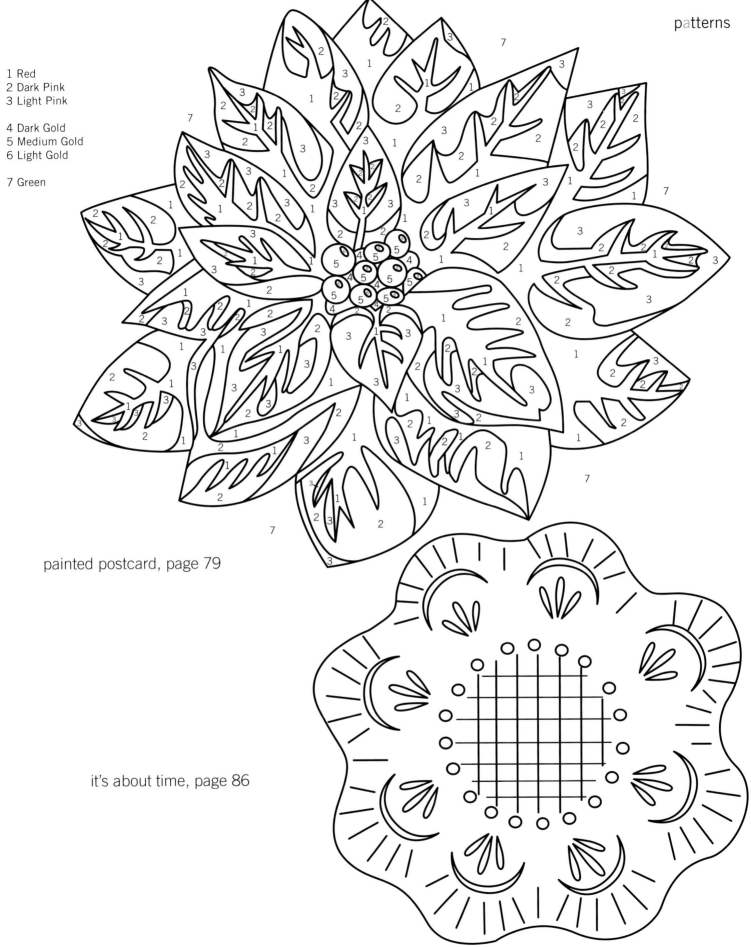

1 Red
2 Dark Pink
3 Light Pink

4 Dark Gold
5 Medium Gold
6 Light Gold

7 Green

painted postcard, page 79

it's about time, page 86

Inside:
1 can sweetened condensed milk
7 1/2 oz. package of coconut
1 tsp. vanilla extract

1/2 cup margarine, melted
1 cup chopped nuts

Chocolate mixture:
Melt 6 oz. semi-sweet chocolate chips and 6 oz. chocolate candy coating in a double boiler.

Mix inside ingredients in a large bowl. Add 1 1/2 boxes of powdered sugar and mix well. Refrigerate for several hours. Shape into small balls. Dip in melted chocolate and dry on wax paper. Roll in tin foil squares.

Chocolate Bon-bons

Inside:
1 can sweetened condensed milk
7 1/2 oz. package of coconut
1 tsp. vanilla extract

1/2 cup margarine, melted
1 cup chopped nuts

Chocolate mixture:
Melt 6 oz. semi-sweet chocolate chips and 6 oz. chocolate candy coating in a double boiler.

Mix inside ingredients in a large bowl. Add 1 1/2 boxes of powdered sugar and mix well. Refrigerate for several hours. Shape into small balls. Dip in melted chocolate and dry on wax paper. Roll in tin foil squares.

Chocolate Bon-bons

Inside:
1 can sweetened condensed milk
7 1/2 oz. package of coconut
1 tsp. vanilla extract

1/2 cup margarine, melted
1 cup chopped nuts

Chocolate mixture:
Melt 6 oz. semi-sweet chocolate chips and 6 oz. chocolate candy coating in a double boiler.

Mix inside ingredients in a large bowl. Add 1 1/2 boxes of powdered sugar and mix well. Refrigerate for several hours. Shape into small balls. Dip in melted chocolate and dry on wax paper. Roll in tin foil squares.

Chocolate Bon-bons

Inside:
1 can sweetened condensed milk
7 1/2 oz. package of coconut
1 tsp. vanilla extract

1/2 cup margarine, melted
1 cup chopped nuts

Chocolate mixture:
Melt 6 oz. semi-sweet chocolate chips and 6 oz. chocolate candy coating in a double boiler.

Mix inside ingredients in a large bowl. Add 1 1/2 boxes of powdered sugar and mix well. Refrigerate for several hours. Shape into small balls. Dip in melted chocolate and dry on wax paper. Roll in tin foil squares.

Chocolate Bon-bons

Inside:
1 can sweetened condensed milk
7 1/2 oz. package of coconut
1 tsp. vanilla extract

1/2 cup margarine,
1 cup chopped nuts

Chocolate Bon-bons

l condensed milk
e of coconut
tract

1/2 cup margarine, melted
1 cup chopped nuts

Chocolate Bon-bons

1 CAN SWEETENED CONDENSED MILK
7 1/2 OZ. PACKAGE OF COCONUT
1 TSP. VANILLA EXTRACT

1/2 CUP MARGARINE, MELTED
1 CUP CHOPPED NUTS

CHOCOLATE MIXTURE:
MELT 6 OZ. SEMI-SWEET CHOCOLATE CHIPS AND 6 OZ. CHOCOLATE CANDY COATING IN A DOUBLE BOILER.

MIX INSIDE INGREDIENTS IN A LARGE BOWL. ADD 1 1/2 BOXES OF POWDERED SUGAR AND MIX WELL. REFRIGERATE FOR SEVERAL HOURS. SHAPE INTO SMALL BALLS. DIP IN MELTED CHOCOLATE AND DRY ON WAX PAPER. ROLL IN TIN FOIL SQUARES.

Chocolate Bon-bons

Inside:
1 can sweetened condensed milk
7 1/2 oz. package of coconut
1 tsp. vanilla extract

1/2 cup margarine, melted
1 cup chopped nuts

Chocolate mixture:
Melt 6 oz. semi-sweet chocolate chips and 6 oz. chocolate candy

Chocolate Bon-bons

Inside:
1 can sweetened condensed milk
7 1/2 oz. package of coconut
1 tsp. vanilla extract

Chocolate mixture:
Melt 6 oz. semi-sweet chocolate chips and 6 oz. chocolate candy coating in a double boiler.

Mix inside ingredients in a large bowl. Add 1 1/2 boxes of powdered sugar and mix well. Refrigerate for several hours. Shape into small balls. Dip in melted chocolate and dry on wax paper. Roll in tin foil squares.

1/2 cup margarine, melted
1 cup chopped nuts

Chocolate

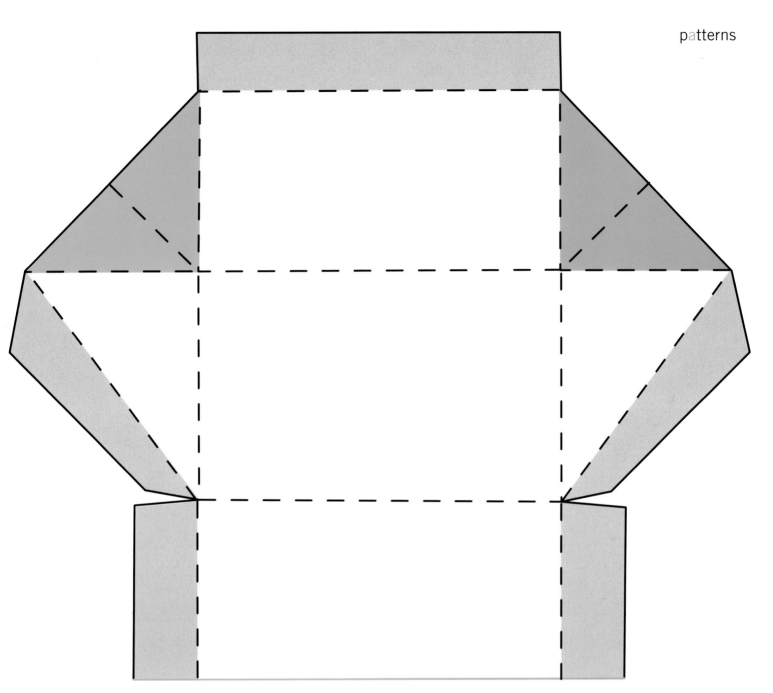

pizzelles' box, page 100

double dipping allowed, page 96

happy christmas

For everyone at Leisure Arts, creating this book has been a labor of love. We want to thank the generous companies who contributed their fine products, helping us make *trimmings* a truly special publication. Merry Christmas to one and all!

Our warmest thanks go to:
❈ Clover Needlecraft, Inc. *www.clover-usa.com* for felting needle tools.
❈ DonJer Products Corporation *www.donjer.com* for Soft Flock® fibers and adhesive.
❈ Creative Paperclay® Company, Inc. *www.creativepaperclay.com* for Paperclay.
❈ Saral® Paper Corporation *www.saralpaper.com* for graphite transfer paper.
❈ USArtQuest, Inc. *www.usartquest.com* for mica flakes.
❈ Royal & Langnickel Brush Mfg., Inc. *www.royalbrush.com* for paintbrushes.
❈ Delta Technical Coatings, Inc. *www.deltacrafts.com* for acrylic paints.